The Miracle of the Loaves and Fishes

Mark 6:30-46, *John* 6:1-15

Retold by Pamela Broughton
Illustrated by Pamela Ford Johnson

A GOLDEN BOOK® • NEW YORK

Copyright © 1999 Golden Books Publishing Company, Inc. Illustrations © 1986 by Pamela Ford Johnson. All rights reserved. Printed in the U.S.A. No part of this book may be reproduced or copied in any form without written permission from the publisher. GOLDEN BOOKS®, A GOLDEN BOOK®, and G DESIGN® are trademarks of Golden Books Publishing Company, Inc., New York, New York, 10106.

One time, Jesus sent out his disciples to teach people and heal people far and wide.

When the disciples returned, they wanted to tell Jesus what they had done and taught while they were away.

But the town was crowded and noisy, and the disciples had not had time to eat.

Jesus said, "Let us go to a quiet place and rest awhile."

So they rowed across the Sea of Galilee to a quiet place.

The people saw Jesus leaving. They saw where he was going, and took a shorter way to the quiet place.

When Jesus reached the other shore, people were already gathered there.

The people seemed like lost sheep. Jesus knew that they needed him to be their shepherd. So he healed those who were sick, and he comforted those who were unhappy.

Then Jesus went up on a mountain with his disciples.

He looked down and saw that there were many, many people in the crowd.

It grew late. Jesus said, "Give them something to eat."

The disciple Philip said, "Two hundred silver coins would not buy enough food for all of them."

The disciples thought Jesus would send them to buy food in the nearby villages.

But Jesus said, "How much food is there? Go and see."

The disciple Andrew answered, "There is a boy with five loaves of barley bread and two small fishes. But how can we feed so many people with so little food?"

Jesus said, "Make the people sit down."
The disciples told the people to sit down in the green grass. There were about five thousand men in the crowd, and many women and children.

Jesus took the five loaves and two fishes. He looked up to heaven. Then he blessed the loaves and broke them. He handed the pieces to his disciples to give to the people.

The fishes, too, were broken and given to the people.

And though it was only a little, and the crowd was huge, there was plenty for everyone after Jesus blessed the food.

When the people had eaten their fill, Jesus told his disciples to gather up the leftover pieces of bread and fish.

They filled twelve big baskets with the pieces that were left after everyone had eaten.

The people wondered at the miracle Jesus had done, feeding so many people with so little food.

Jesus sent the people away.

Then he told his disciples to row back across the sea.

Jesus said he would come to them later. And he went alone up the mountain to pray.